The Canadian Rockies
PANORAMAS

The pristine wilderness to enjoy respect and preserve

Photographs and text by

GEORGE BRYBYCIN

❀❀❀❀❀❀❀❀❀❀ G B PUBLISHING ❀❀❀❀❀❀❀❀❀❀❀❀

Photographic studies by George Brybycin:

The High Rockies

Colourful Calgary

Our Fragile Wilderness

The Rocky Mountains

Banff National Park

Jasper National Park

Colourful Calgary II

Wildlife in the Rockies

Rocky Mountain Symphony

Enchanted Wilderness

Wilderness Odyssey

Rocky Mountain Symphony II

Romance of the Rockies

Calgary - The Sunshine City

The Living Rockies

Cosmopolitan Calgary

Banff and Jasper N.P.

The Rockies: Wildlife

The Majestic Rockies

Emerald Waters of the Rockies

The Canadian Rockies Panoramas

Text Editor: Sheldon Wiebe
Design: George Brybycin
Printed and bound in Singapore by
Kim Hup Lee Printing Co Pte Limited

ISBN 0-919029-21-3 Paperback

For current list, please write to:

GB PUBLISHING, Box 6292, Station D,
Calgary, Alberta Canada T2P 2C9

If you love this still beautiful planet and all of its many wonders (including humanity), then adapt these simple ideas for your lifestyle:

- Respect and protect nature and our environment.
- Educate your family and friends about environmental issues.
- Support environmental organizations - buy memberships.
- Plant a tree, or two or ten, in your yard and have your own miniature forest with birds and squirrels, and all the nature sights, sounds and smells they bring.
- Remember that one tree absorbs 4.5 kilograms of carbon monoxide per year. Hug a tree, it cleans the air you breathe - it is your friend.
- If a tree is exposed to 20 kilograms of pollutants a year, it will sicken and die (in just the same way that people exposed to radiation sicken and die).
- When you hike in the wilderness - pack your trash out.
- Admire the intricate beauty of a wild flower, but never pick it - flowers must mature in order to produce seeds and reproduce.
- In areas where there are sidewalks - use them! Grass breathes carbon dioxide and produces oxygen. Do not destroy it.
- Hunt only if you need the meat for food. Too many species have become endangered as a result of hunting for pleasure.
- Buy a synthetic Christmas tree and use it for thirty years. If we all did this, think of the real trees we could save.
- Recycle. Recycle. Recycle. Use both sides of all paper; use the same shopping bag until it begins to wear out (then use it as a garbage bag); return all deposit products for refunds. Every little bit helps.
- Overly packaged, or disposable products create non-biodegradable landfill. Avoid them at all costs.
- Buy carefully. More and more environmentally friendly products are available all the time. Use them.
- Think before you do… Make the environmentally wise decision.
- Rid yourself of greed and materialism.
- Vote for political candidates who run "green" campaigns. And if they get elected, hold them to their "green" campaign promises.
- Avoid smoking. Not only does it cause cancer, but it deadens the senses and shortens the breath. And the smells of nature are not to be missed.
- Drink less today than you did yesterday. Drinking alcohol kills brain cells and deadens the senses.
- Drugs? Drugs are deceptive, extremely addictive, they kill the will and deaden the senses (do you sense a trend here)?
- Be kind, friendly and gentle. Compassion and kindness are never embarrassing, even for professional athletes.

Remember, we will all continue to be healthy and alive only as long as we help Mother Nature to be the same.
I ask that you will understand what I am saying.
Will you? Please?

The Canadian Rockies
PANORAMAS

A collection of 62 fine, large format photographs featuring the rich diversity of subjects to be found in the Canadian Rocky Mountains.

The main features of this book are large open vistas and panoramas unique to the Canadian Rockies. The rich diversity of mountain landscapes is presented in vivid color and large format. Popular landmarks and other destinations, out-of-the-way places, wild and remote areas, breathtaking high altitude views and some mountain flora and fauna are presented for your pleasure.

Please remember that the Rockies (or any wilderness, for that matter), will only remain pristine, green and beautiful when humans limit their activities to visiting. Wilderness and civilization do not mix well.

❀ ❀ ❀ ❀ ❀ ❀ ❀ ❀ ❀ ❀ ❀ ❀ ❀

*The eastern part of the Valley of the Ten Peaks, a classic
of the Rockies. Banff National Park.*

*Banff Springs Hotel - this grand Victorian landmark blends well into
the wilderness of Sulphur Mountain. Banff National Park.*

The fabulous Lake Louise, Mt. Victoria and red poppies in front of the Chateau. Banff National Park.

A spectacular mountain paradise: the Valley of the Ten Peaks. Banff National Park.

The monumental Storm Mountain (3161 m.) and the forests of Bow Valley viewed on a crisp autumn morning. Banff National Park.

This school outing introduces youngsters to the great and healthy outdoors - perhaps enchanting them for life. Paradise Valley. Banff National Park.

A pleasant day in early winter by the second Vermilion Lake with the Fairholme Range in the background. Banff National Park.

*A frosty and misty morning near the Kicking Horse Pass
and Mt. Field (2635 m.) Yoho National Park.*

The Red Deer River and the Lakes Valley viewed from Fossil Mountain. Note the Cyclone Group in the background. Banff National Park.

*The alpine meadows west of Healy Pass, along the trail
to Egypt Lake. Banff National Park.*

Kananaskis Country: endless forests, flower-carpeted meadows - a naturalist's delight. The Mt. Foch/Mt. Sorrail Group on the horizon.

*Banff's principal landmark, Mt. Rundle (2998 m.) was named for Methodist missionary
Robert T.Rundle, who viewed the mountain in 1847. Banff National Park.*

*Like a dream castle straight from Hans Christian Anderson's fairy tale, Chateau Lake Louise
is surrounded by a winter wonderland. Lake Louise, Banff National Park.*

The juniors run for fame and glory in one of many racing categories in the annual ski races staged at Lake Louise. Banff National Park.

A "bird's-eye view" of autumnish Lake Minnewanka, photographed from the summit of Cascade Mountain (2998 m.) Banff National Park.

Spectacular Hector Lake is located at the east end of the Wapta Icefield, the silt from which creates the emerald color of the water. Photographed from Mt. Hector (3394 m.) Banff National Park.

A view of the Simpson River Valley and the Mitchell Range from
Quartz Hill (2580 m.) Kootenay National Park.

Even in late August, last winter's snow provides meltwater for lush meadows near Citadel Pass. Banff National Park.

A Christmas tree in front of the monumental Banff Springs Hotel. Banff National Park.

A seldom photographed "back face" of the Chateau Lake Louise. Banff National Park.

*Winter sets in around Peyto Lake, named after early guide
and adventurer, Bill Peyto. Banff National Park.*

*Bow Glacier and the Wapta Icefield, above Bow Falls. The birthplace
of the Bow River. Banff National Park.*

*The highest of them all, Mt. Robson (3954 m.) is the Monarch
of the Canadian Rockies. Mt. Robson Provincial Park.*

*The jagged Cathedral Crags (3073 m.) a well-known landmark located by
the Spiral Tunnel, near the town of Field. Yoho National Park.*

This is how the High Rockies look - a truly awesome view from
Mt. Temple (3547 m.) to the south. Banff National Park.

*A splendid view from Mt. Richardson (3086 m.) facing north-east. Lake Merlin
and the Wall of Jericho are in the center. Banff National Park.*

*In the fall, Elk (Cervus elaphus) gather in large herds during rutting season. When the season
is over, adult cows and their young and yearlings form small groups. Young bulls
stay together, while the adult bulls tend to become solitary.*

Bighorn Sheep (Ovis canadensis) commonly found throughout the Rockies.

The Timber Wolf (Canis lupus) is the largest Canidae in temperate North America.

Colorful mountain meadows along the Dolomite Pass trail. The best flower-viewing time is August.
Depending on the weather, it may last up to fifteen days.

*A pleasant view from Fossil Mountain (2946 m.) facing south. Below is Baker Lake
and the Sawback Range forms the background.*

*Starry, starry night...a time exposure of star tracks and faint Northern Lights
in the northwestern skies over Bow Lake. Banff National Park.*

The elusive and hard to photograph Northern Lights over the northern part of Banff National Park.

One of the many streams coming from the glaciated north side of Mt. Edith Cavell. Jasper National Park.

*White-water rafting on a wild and spectacular Maligne River (above and left). A wilderness adventure
to remember for a lifetime. Jasper National Park abounds in wildlife, rich flora
and fine mountain scenery, with plenty of space for all.*

The western part of the Wapta Icefield viewed at sunrise from Mistaya Mountain (3078 m.).
On the left, below Peyto Peak, Caldron Lake can be seen. Banff National Park.

On the summit of Mt. Burgess (2599 m.) On the left horizon is snowy Mt. Vaux of the Ottertail Range.
On the right is Mt. King of the Van Horne Range. Yoho National Park.

*Golden autumn, blue-clear Alberta skies by fortress-like Castle Mountain
(2766 m.) a major landmark of Banff National Park.*

*Bronzed by the rising sun, monumental Castle Mountain (2766 m.) dominates
the wintry Bow Valley. A very scenic site in Banff National Park.*

A colorful patio in front of Chateau Lake Louise is a perfect place to refresh oneself on a hot summer day. Banff National Park.

Not many of the world's grand hotels can match location, ambience and services of Chateau Lake Louise. Banff National Park.

This is Banff, in all its majesty. A world-renowned mountain resort, Banff offers all major tourist attractions, three superb ski areas nearby, world-class hotels, restaurants and great shopping.

*A night image of the resort town of Banff and its environs. Mt. Rundle dominates the scene,
Second Vermilion Lake is in the middle with the busy Trans-Canada
Highway traversing the scene. Banff National Park.*

The Engelmann spruce and golden larch forest around picturesque
Elizabeth Lake. Mount Assiniboine Provincial Park.

Yellow lady's slipper (Cypripedium calceolus).

Wild rose (Rosa woodsii).

*Looking at this picture taken from the summit of Mt. Hector (3394 m.), one wouldn't hesitate to call
this God's Country. The gorgeous emerald Hector Lake, lush green Bow Valley
and the endless vistas of the majestic Rockies. Banff National Park.*

A winter camp along the trail to Mt. Assiniboine, near Citadel Pass (2352 m.). The Simpson River Valley and the Mitchell Range form the background. Kootenay National Park.

The ever busy and expanding Banff Springs Hotel Complex as seen from Tunnel Mountain. Banff National Park.

The town of Banff's main thoroughfare - Banff Avenue, with Cascade Mountain in the background. Banff National Park.

Moraine Lake. Banff National Park. Easily accessible by car in the summer, it is a different story come winter. It is a 26 kilometers return trip to view this splendid place in its tranquil winter majesty - and well worth the effort.

The pristine glory of new snow transforms the Valley of the Ten Peaks into a peaceful winter wonderland. Banff National Park.

*The legendary beauty of Moraine Lake defies description. An early morning
visit guarantees enchantment. Banff National Park.*

*Beautifully landscaped gardens and flowerbeds in front
of Chateau Lake Louise. Banff National Park.*

For climbers only. An immense panorama from Mt. Temple (3547 m.) Banff National Park. In the foreground, clockwise: Mt. Bell, Consolation Pass, Bident Mountain, Mt. Quadra, Mt. Babel and Mt. Fay. Middle ground: Storm Mountain, Mt. Ball and Stanley Peak. On the horizon, poking through the morning mist, Mt. Sir Douglas and Mt. Assiniboine can be recognized.

The author bivouacked on the summit of Mt. Temple (3547 m.) in the hole on the right. Two climbers bivouacked on the north wall near the summit. Soon after sunrise they appeared on the summit, greeting George with: "Are you real?" The view is to the southwest and in the center is the Horseshoe Glacier, below the Hungabee Mountain.

*Looking northwest toward the Ball Range from Healy Pass. Egypt
and Scarab Lakes are on the left. Banff National Park.*

The Tonquin Valley, Amethyst Lake and the Ramparts. This alpine paradise abounds in rich flora and fauna, including grizzly bear, wolf, wolverine and mountain caribou. Jasper National Park.

One of the most attractive lakes, Maligne Lake has it all: rich flora and fauna, beautiful mountains, serene shores, scenic hiking trails, good fishing and boating. Reflected in the lake are Mt. Charlton (3217 m.) on the left and Mt. Unwin (3268 m.) Jasper National Park.

The Dome Glacier descends from the Columbia Icefield between The Snow Dome and Mt. Kitchener and is reflected in a small mountain tarn. Exploring glaciers is very dangerous because of hidden crevasses and only well-equipped parties should think of trying it. Jasper National Park.

Bighorn Sheep (Ovis canadensis) are quite common in the Rockies. They are often seen along the road "begging" for handouts. Feeding any wild animal is unlawful and contributes to the killing of many beautiful animals by cars. Please, do not attempt to feed wildlife.